Emotionally Yours

Dr. Heet N. Desai

First Published in January 2022

ISBN: 978-93-93388-33-9

BLUEROSE PUBLISHERS

www.bluerosepublishers.com
info@bluerosepublishers.com
+91 8882 898 898

Cover Design:
Aveek

Typographic Design:
Rohit

Distributed by: BlueRose, Amazon, Flipkart

Table of Contents

LOVE IS A LANGUAGE

• • •

I AM YOURS

I'll remain yours with my every breath,
Till my life goes on,
As God has sent me in this world for you,
And it's only for you that I'm born..

Even when I'm far away,
No matter how long may be the distance,
Whenever you need me,
I'll be there for you at that very instance..

If you find yourself in the dark,
I'll become your light,
And any problem that you face in your life,
I promise to be the soldier in your fight..

You are the pole star of my life,
That always helps me in finding my way,
And you just keep running over my mind,
Every single night and day..

I strongly feel I can't live without you,
None of my day passes by without you in it,
Because since the time you have entered my life,
My life has become like a movie super hit..

I'll always belong to you,
You have captured me with your charming force,
And one thing I want to let you know,
That I was, I am, and I'll always be yours..

Your presence in this world,
Has turned everything new,
And every second my heart whispers,
That I love you..

\- Heet N. Desai

ANGEL ON EARTH

You came in my life as a beautiful dream,
Taking away my breath and soul,
My heart started beating for you,
Not in pieces, but as a whole…

This mysterious night reveals so many stories,
Telling me about your beauty,
I said I am already aware of your charm,
It replied 'I am just obeying my duty…'

You are like a cool evening during summer time,
Just so delightful and so calm,
Your lovely smile plays with your lips,
Just like grazing grains in a farm…

The spark in your eyes is brighter than the stars,
Everything about you seems so perfect,
Time stops for a while when you smile,
Even the nature agrees to this fact…

You are always there for me,
No matter near or far,
I was just like a setting sun,
You made me a rising star…

You are the most beautiful girl,
And would be so for many more births,
That's the reason my heart whispers,
"You are an angel on earth!!"

- Heet N. Desai

WHEN

When the sun cannot rise,
And stars refuse to glow,
When the moon stops appearing,
And the wind refuses to blow;
When sorrows don't exist,
And 'problem' is just a word,
When a heart never cries,
And screams cannot be heard;
When the sky and land merges,
And time stops forever,
When the flowers refuse to blossom,
And misunderstandings occur never;
When the birds cannot fly,
And plants cannot grow,
When a fish cannot swim,
And water cannot flow;
When a day is of 30 hours,
And a year has 13 months,
When a genius cannot answer,
And a hunter cannot hunt;
When fights cannot be fought,
And songs cannot be sung,
When tears never roll down,
And hearts cannot be won…

When all these things happen,
When all of it finally comes true,
That day, without a doubt,
I'll stop loving you…

- Heet N. Desai

YOUR EYES...

In your eyes is the place where I see my world,
In your eyes I can see my life getting whorled;
In your eyes is a night full of stars,
In your eyes are present love filled jars;
In your eyes is hidden a beautiful smile,
In your eyes when I drown time stops for a while;
In your eyes is a maze which has no way out,
In your eyes is a voice that speaks very loud;
In your eyes is a river that swiftly flows,
In your eyes is a spark that always glows;
In your eyes is a garden full of flowers,
In your eyes I get lost for seconds, minutes, hours;
In your eyes resides a beautiful dream,
In your eyes is shouting a silent scream;
In your eyes is a home where dwells love,
In your eyes is the heaven that is present above;
In your eyes is the weapon which has the power to kill,
In your eyes is the sunset seen from the top of the hill;
In your eyes roars the mighty ocean,
In your eyes I can see all the emotions;
In your eyes is the reaction that cannot be reversed,
In your eyes I can see the whole universe;

In your eyes whatever I can I see,
Are all the things in this nature which can be…

\- Heet N. Desai

THE UNCONDITIONAL PROMISE

I promise to be there for you,
Whenever you need me;
I promise to be there for you,
No matter what the condition be...

I promise to be there for you,
To share all your problems;
I promise to be there for you,
With your heart just whisper my name...

I promise to be there for you,
Throughout the span of life;
I promise to be there for you,
Even if into your sorrows I have to dive...

I promise to be there for you,
To catch your rolling tears;
I promise to be there for you,
And chase away all your fears...

I promise to be there for you,
And turn your world brighter than the sun,
I promise to be there for you,
Even when you just need someone to listen...

I promise to fulfill all these promises,
Filling your life with happiness and glee;
And trust me when I say,
For you I'll always be…

- Heet N. Desai

MILES TOGETHER

We have traversed quite a distance so far,
But still it seems so less,
Like it had been just yesterday,
When we had started from rest…

I still remember when we first began,
Taking every step so carefully,
And although there were thorns along the path,
We walked through them successfully…

Crawling was how it all started,
Till we were able to walk tall and high,
Making ourselves capable of jumping,
Till in the free air we could finally fly…

We came across happiness and sorrows,
We came across nostalgic memories,
We spent every moment with smile on our faces,
And moved just like cool and calm breeze…

Life directed us to our destiny,
And we followed it just like a couple of shadows,
Swimming in the ocean of dreams,
No matter whether deep or shallow…

Thank you for always being by my side,
on or away from the shore,
And I promise in this journey of life,
I'll be with you for many a miles more…

\- Heet N. Desai

ANOTHER DAY BEGINS

As the sun rays fall on my eyes,
I am drawn out of my sleep,
Everything around appears so bright and new,
As if I was just lying next to you..

The cool and fresh morning breeze,
Carries with it your fragrance,
And in the melodies chirping of birds,
Your soft and sweet voice can be heard..

The clear sunny sky of afternoon,
Seems to depict your pretty face,
Showing the sparkle and glow you possess,
Even the nature, with you, seems to be so obsessed..

Then comes the pleasant time of evening,
Surroundings appear so cool and calm,
Just like your precious innocent heart,
From where beauty can never part..

The sun has just gone down the horizon,
And the beautiful dusk covers the sky,
But its beauty is nothing compared to you,
I know you won't agree, but it is quite true..

The night sets in and stars begin to peep,
Searching for an angel on earth,
And then, finally you come in their sight,
Completing their search in this beautiful night..

This is how a day passes,
Making every moment so special,
And as this long day finally ends,
Tomorrow, another day begins..

- Heet N. Desai

A PLACE CALLED HEART

A place where Deep Ocean of secrets dwell,
From where love never parts,
Where angels preserve their wise virtues,
That's the place called heart..

Though it's quite a small place,
The world can be explored in it,
Where the immense beauty of a person is seen,
And where candles of hope are lit..

It is the place where silence screams,
Where light of joy never fades,
Where souls find a place to relax,
And where memories give their enchanting shades..

The words which we are unable to convey,
Are expressed by the heart in its own way,
And when it is overwhelmed by emotions,
How it feels, the tears say..

The special thing about this heart,
Is that it never believes in quitting,
You give it a thousand reasons to stop,
It will still give you one for beating..

Where feelings take their unique shapes,
And life creates its beautiful art,
Where the truth of every person prevails,
That's the place called heart..

\- Heet N. Desai

LIFE LONG

In life, people come and go,
Moments are shared and memories are formed,
But you are not among those people,
Because you'll be with me forever life long..

Its hardly been a few months since we met,
But somehow I feel I know you since ages,
My life is like an open book for you,
And you are filling its pages..

You are the sun that never sets,
Making my day shine,
And I hope you'll always remember,
Without you my life wont be fine..

At night when the stars twinkle above,
It reminds me of you,
Because you are the rising star of the nature,
And people like you are very few..

Beautiful night and dazzling lights,
Decorate the entire city,
And I believe no matter what,
You'll be with me till eternity...

Mountains are shouting,
And birds are singing songs,
That I'll always be there for you,
And you'll be with me forever life long..

- Heet N. Desai

RAINBOW BETWEEN HEARTS

Rainbow is a pretty beautiful sight,
Right from the very moment it starts,
But it looks even more beautiful,
When it bridges two hearts..

In nature, it occurs after rains,
Its appearance is so charming and neat,
But between two hearts it occurs,
When the two hearts finally meet..

It communicates feelings and emotions,
It makes our heartbeats run,
And so strong is its bond,
That it makes the two hearts one..

Each color of this rainbow,
Carries a beautiful meaning,
Expressing its very importance,
And how perfect it is its revealing..

Let's begin with the color VIOLET,
Signifying magic and mystery,
It says how precisely the two hearts,
Develop their magical chemistry..

Moving to the color INDIGO,
It represents deep midnight sky,
When the whole world is asleep,
Those two little hearts are preparing to fly..

Then comes the color BLUE,
Associated with faithfulness,
The strongest bond it is supposed to be,
Between the hearts in truthfulness..

GREEN is the next color,
Representing prosperity,
The two hearts once bonded,
Are never separated till the day after eternity..

Next is the color YELLOW,
It symbolizes wisdom,
Showing if wisdom prevails in both the hearts,
Misunderstandings occur quite seldom..

We move on to color ORANGE,
It means vitality with endurance,
The two hearts always stand for each other,
No matter how long may be the distance..

Finally we come to color RED,
We all know its importance,
Representing the bond of love between two hearts,
And this love increases every instance..

So that's the reason I say..

Rainbow is a pretty beautiful sight,
Lovely are all its parts,
But it looks even more beautiful,
When this rainbow is between two hearts..

- Heet N. Desai

WHERE ANGELS DWELL…

You come from a place where angels dwell,
A place where happiness flows like a river,
A place away from this mortal world,
A place where beauty resides always and forever…

You come from a place where angels dwell,
A place beyond all rights and wrongs,
A place where only peace prevails,
A place unbounded of all rules and norms…

You come from a place where angels dwell,
A place where the skies are always blue,
A place beyond the horizon,
A place where every day springs turn new…

You come from a place where angels dwell,
A place where fields are green,
A place where the sea has waves of emotions,
A place where the storm of love is so pure and clean…

You come from a place where angels dwell,
A place where the land is as soft as birds' feathers,

A place where resides prosperity,
A place where day and night live together…

You come from a place where angels dwell,
A place lying amidst the stars,
A place where butterflies drift across the wind,
A place which is, from this world, very far…

That is the place you come from,
And you are more precious than the rarest jewel,
You are quite different from these mortal souls,
Because you come from a place where angels dwell…

- Heet N. Desai

THIS WORLD IS NOT ENOUGH

So many things in this world,
Can be dedicated to you,
But how to describe you in words,
I have no clue..

To compare you with sky,
Just does not seem to be right,
Because the sky is just a base for you,
And you are much above its height..

To compare you with stars,
Does not feel to be fine,
Because the glow those stars possess,
Is just a small part of your shine..

Lets try and compare you with the ocean,
But wait, even that's not good enough,
Because to compare your vast abilities with just an ocean,
I find it to be a little tough..

People say you are a piece of moon,
Well, that isn't something new for you,
But for me the case is somewhat different,

Because I feel the beautiful moon is just a part of you..

Even the roses in the garden are jealous of you,
Because you are more beautiful than them,
And even the rarest diamond is afraid of you,
Because it feels that you'll prove to be a better gem..

So as you can clearly see,
To compare you with all these things is becoming so tough,
And if there's truly something which can be dedicated to you,
Then this world is just not enough..

- Heet N. Desai

JUST HOLD MY HAND

Just hold my hand,
And forget your fright,
Just hold my hand,
Till everything seems right..

Just hold my hand,
And guide me through the way,
Just hold my hand,
Till the end of the day..

Just hold my hand,
And fill my lonely hours,
Just hold my hand,
Till we reach the stars..

Just hold my hand,
And fly like a bird,
Just hold my hand,
Till our silence can be heard..

Just hold my hand,
And close your eyes,
Just hold my hand,
Till the truth takes over lies..

Just hold my hand,
And drown in the ocean of love,
Just hold my hand,
Till this ocean flows in my every nerve..

Just hold my hand,
And I'll get healed,
Just hold my hand,
And my every pain will be killed..

Just hold my hand,
And keep holding it tighter,
Just hold my hand,
And my days will be brighter..

Just hold my hand,
And everything will turn new,
Just hold my hand,
And you'll realize how much I Love You..

- Heet N. Desai

JUST LIKE A FAIRYTALE

Under the dim light of the lonely moon,
I fell asleep on the bed of stars,
And then I entered a world resembling fairyland,
A place completely different from ours..

There, I met a girl having fairy like appearances,
Maybe she was the fairy herself,
As this place was completely unknown to me,
She agreed to offer me her help..

Although she was a stranger to me,
I felt her to be someone known,
Maybe because her beauty had captured me,
Maybe because of the qualities she owned..

She took me on the journey of her fairyland,
On a marvelous gigantic unicorn,
The tall grasses of the field were kissing our feet,
And the wind was greeting the crown that she had
worn..

She showed me some of the breathtaking places,
Lake of wine, magical valleys, sky touching
mountains and a pearl filled ocean,
This almost appeared to be something fictitious,

And sighing them was so much fun..

Finally we came to the place from where we had started,
And she told me that she had to go,
Although my waving hand was giving her farewell,
My heart was shouting "Please don't go!"

Something in my soul forced me to call her back,
She listened, turned and I ran to her,
Maybe my heart had started beating for her,
And that I wanted to convey to her..

When those magical words had reached my lips,
And they were just about to leap,
There rang my morning alarm,
And I was out of my sleep..

- Heet N. Desai

BEYOND INFINITY

Even when the oceans run out of their waters,
I'll still be there with you,
Even when the mighty sun loses its fire,
I'll still be there with you...

Even when the stars disappear from the sky,
I'll still be there with you,
Even when the moon no longer lightens the night,
I'll still be there with you...

Even when this world comes down,
I'll still be there with you,
Even after we cross the line of eternity,
I'll still be there with you...

Even after our souls leave our bodies,
I'll still be there with you,
Even after we complete thus journey of life,
I'll still be there with you...

Even when the birds no longer chirp,
I'll still be there with you,
Even when the rains cease to fall,
I'll still be there with you...

Even when no one is beside you when your soul embarks,
I'll still be there with you when you get into the dark,
Even when the heartbeat leaves the heart,
I'll still be there with you and never go apart...

If even there are thousand miles between us when you need me,
Just walk the first one and I'll walk the rest just to be with you,
But promise me that you'll never go away,
Because without you even the heaven is of no use…

- Heet N. Desai

MEET ME IN THE STARS

Every night as I go off to my bed,
Thoughts of you keep running through my head,
When the whispers of soft breeze of air reaches my ears,
My heart feels that you are here..

But you actually are many miles away,
And I hope to see you every another day,
So when the night together, can't be ours,
Just close your eyes and meet me in the stars..

There I will be, waiting for you,
With a bottle of wine, and glasses for two,
So just close your eyes, and come up there,
Forgetting all the sorrows and despair..

I wait among the stars, lost in your thoughts,
A beautiful night I have planned for you in this very plot,
I see a blurry image behind that cloud,
And in front of this image even the stars have bowed..

As the cloud moves away, the image gets clear,
And there you are, right in front of me, so near,
I drag you closer and the music begins to play,

You look so beautiful, I have no words to say..

As the music advances, we begin to dance,
I had waited so long for this precious chance,
This gentle music is filled with so much romance,
The whole place lighted by stars, no boundaries, no fence..

So just close your eyes and there you'll see,
A special place in the stars just for you and me,
Just meet me in the stars; from all the worldly grieves you'll be free,
Waiting in the stars for you, I promise I will be!!

- Heet N. Desai

BECAUSE I ASKED HEAVEN

With every day passing by,
My love for you rises high,
Just like an angel sent from paradise,
You changed my life with a blink of your eyes..

I see us walking in a garden full of roses,
Lost in your dreams my long night dozes,
Maybe we were destined to meet someway and somehow,
That's the reason we are so close right now..

I see us sharing our happiness and pain,
The moments we share run in my every vein,
I just want time to stay still forever,
So that even time can part us never..

I thank God everyday for sending me you,
For you'd never lie to me and always stay true,
I always dreamt of a world where it's just you and I,
And together we see the life passing by..

If there ever comes a time when we have to part,
I swear to be true, you'll still possess my heart,
Just like a soul never lies the body till the person dies,

I'll always be there for you and devastate your dark
times with light..

So now I am down on my knees with my face towards
the sky,
Seeing the bright stars in this beautiful night,
Hoping that someday my dreams will come true,
Because I asked heaven if I could have you!!

- Heet N. Desai

A BEAUTIFUL FRIEND

You came in my life as an unknown face,
Not knowing that our friendship, one day, I would embrace,
But now whenever I think about the talks with you,
It brings me big smiles and laughter too..

Thank you for being so gentle and kind,
People like you are really hard to find,
Thank you for trusting me right from the start,
You truly possess a wonderful heart..

Our friendship means a lot to me,
I only hope that this I can make you see,
And I promise that in times of need,
I'll be the best friend anyone can possibly be..

I'll always be there to support you,
I'll help you fight your fears too,
And I know when I feel down you'll give me a lift,
You truly are an extraordinary gift..

I am lucky enough to have met you,
And I thank God for gifting me this friendship so new,
I love the unique bond that you and I possess,

And somehow you never fail to impress..

Even though it's only a little time that we shared,
I could see that you really care,
And our friendship isn't something that can be bought or sold,
I value it more than a mountain of gold..

If this world would comprise of more people like you,
Happiness will dominate and no one will be blue,
You seem like an angel the heaven has sent,
And we'll always be friends, till the very end!

- Heet N. Desai

YOU AND I…

You are the words, I am the action,
You are the path, I am the direction..
You are the cry, I am the weep,
You are the dream, I am the sleep..
You are the cure, I am the pain,
You are the cloud, I am the rain,
You are a poem; I am a plain sheet,
You are the heart, I am the beat..
You are the eye, I am the tear,
You are the strength, I am the fear..
You are interesting, I am a bore,
You are the ocean, I am the shore..
You are silent, I am loud,
You are the answer, I am the doubt,
You are the Spring of March; I am the summer of May,
You are a beautiful eclipse, I am just a normal day..
You are a treasure; I am a single coin,
You are a palace, I am a quoin..
You are the sea, I am a bay,
You are the night, I am the day..
You are the star, I am a meteorite,
You are the sun, I am the light..
You are the destiny, I am the fate; I'm yours and you are my soul-mate

\- Heet N. Desai

THE STORY OF 14TH FEB!

Every star is twinkling so brightly tonight,
Even the nature is not ready to stay quiet,
Everyone out there are humming the melody of love,
Whether you talk about the mighty mountains or free flying doves...

On this special occasion of Valentine's day,
There are so many things that my heart wants to say,
From where should I start I have no clue,
But be it anything, everything's going to start and end with you...

You know that I love you more than words can say,
You are like the shining sun in my lonely day,
In your praise even the words in the dictionary are few,
Seems like Cupid has hit his arrows on us too..

Your presence in my life is just like a treat,
And sometimes you make my heart skip a beat,
You are the one, who softly speaks to my heart,
And believe me, there exists no force that can make us apart...

With you even a street of thorns seems like a red carpet,
Within your lovely eyes my happiness is guarded,
Tonight forget your fright and just let love take over,
Till our eyes start to blink slower..

And when you fall asleep I'll meet you in your dreams,
Just like a small fairy tale it will seem,
So tonight, waiting with two glasses and a bottle of wine,
I want to ask you, will you be my Valentine?

- Heet N. Desai

A MOMENT OF TRUTH

Waking up with a message from you,
Makes my morning so beautiful,
Sleeping at night after talking to you,
Makes my sleep so peaceful..

You are like the sunshine which brightens my life,
You are like the silence of the night,
You give my heart a priceless joy,
And with your support even with this world I can fight.

You are like a pearl in the depths of an ocean,
Your eyes as bright as the stars in the sky,
Listening to your voice gives a different delight,
You are the dose that makes me high.

I promise that I'll never leave you alone,
I promise to be there with you for every moment of forever,
And when everything else crumbles and falls apart,
I'll still be there with you and go away never.

I hope I can show you how much I care,
I'll be the wall to protect you from all the dangers,
And I promise that in times of need,

I'll take all your pains, for me they are no strangers.

When you feel down I'll make you smile,
I'll try to secure you from all the harm,
I'll promise you all the happiness in this world,
Because for me you are my lucky charm

- Heet N. Desai

THE REASON

Hazy sunlight in the winter mornings,
Feels so comforting and warm,
You act the same in my dark times,
Being there in every way & form...

I fall in love with the feeling I get,
When you slide your soft fingers over my hair,
All the tensions of the world vanishes in a while,
When in your beautiful eyes I begin to stare...

You are the reason I want to wake in the morning,
You are the reason for my peaceful sleep,
If you want to know how much you mean to me,
You'll have to peep into my heart so deep...

Your unconditional and affable nature,
Pleases my brain and heart so well,
And if you are always with me,
It doesn't matter if the place is heaven or hell...

You are the orbit on which my life revolves,
Whenever I'm lost, you are my clue,
And if today I am who I am,
The Reason is only you!

\- Heet N. Desai

IRRESISTIBLE

If you ask me how much I love you,
You'll have to spare years to hear my answer,
Or wait, maybe even decades,
As this love increases every day, every month, every year...

Being someone's first love is an amazing feeling,
But being someone's last is just beyond perfection,
And that's what I want to be for you,
With all the love in my heart and this warm affection...

My life was good even before you entered it,
But it has become better by your presence,
And all the things which were once pointless,
Have all started to make complete sense...

I don't wish to be your whole world,
But I want to be your favorite part of it,
And since the day I have met you,
Thinking about someone else just isn't worth it...

Even if we spend the whole day together,
I'll miss you the very second you leave,
Because we are connected by an enchanting bond,

And I suppose this even you believe...

My heart beats so fast when we are together,
I don't think you have any clue,
Because you bring a new sunrise to my life,
And there's something just so irresistible about you!

- Heet N. Desai

TOGETHER FOREVER

Seven billion people around the globe,
But someday, somewhere I had to meet her,
The day was bright, the sky was blue,
For the first time when I heard her whisper..

Her voice as if a nightingale's song,
The spark in her eyes put the stars to shame,
'Hi, it's a pleasure to meet you', I said,
Reciprocating she told me her name...

Things went fine and smooth between us,
Our relation went in a new direction,
Little did I know how beautiful it would be,
That our relation would be molded with so much perfection...

When I had seen her for the first time,
I thanked God for introducing me to the most beautiful angel,
But if you ask me to describe her beauty in words,
I am sorry because to do that I will be unable...

I knew she was someone very special,
Because she made my heart beat more rapidly,
I used to look at her and smile for no reason,

And I fell for her unexpectedly...

Now that she is leaving from here,
My heart aches that I won't be able to see her for long,
Although the distance between us will keep us away,
She is the one to whom my heart will always belong...

Even if she is leaving now I'm sure about one thing,
That distance doesn't matter for the hearts who really care,
For the moments and memories we share span the miles,
And within a few seconds with each other we are back there!

- Heet N. Desai

YOU ARE THE ONE...

Remember the times when our friendship was new,
Just like the morning grass bathing in dew,
Everything around was filled with happiness and hue,
It was then when I realized I was falling in love with you...

Those late night chats filled with laughter and love,
Even a moment spent with you made my day good enough,
This time I fell so hard and fast,
And I promise my love for you will forever last...

What can I do to make you mine?
Be your shoulder to cry on or shade you from firing sunshine,
What should I do, I have no clue,
How to be the one who enchants you...

You had to come in my life somewhere someday,
And now when you are here I have got no words to say,
Why does this happen when I have so many things to tell,
Why are my lips sealed when my heart wants to yell...

Sometimes the best friendships grow into something more intense,

Breaking all the boundaries and the fence,

What sort of magic did you do?

To make me fall in love with you!

- Heet N. Desai

THE AIR I BREATHE

We come across so many people in our lives,
Some come and go, while some stay for a while,
But among all these people whom we meet,
There are only a few who can be a reason for our smile...

You are not only the reason for my happiness,
But also my reason to live this life,
And there's nothing that I won't do for you,
Even if it calls for walking on the edge of a knife..

Maybe I don't tell you every day,
How much you mean to me,
But I love you more than you can ever imagine,
And I hope this love, in my eyes you can see...

I'll never let go off your hand,
Even if this world goes down, or even if my heart bleeds,
Because as long as you are holding my hand,
There's nothing else that I would need...

I'll always be standing strong by your side,
Even if into your sorrows I have to dive,
Because you made your way into my heart,

Faster than you made your way into my life..

So now I'm on my knees telling this to you,
With heaven above and this earth beneath,
You are the oxygen my heart needs,
You are the air that I breathe...

- Heet N. Desai

IN THE NIGHT WITH ME

This moment in front of us,
Will last till eternity,
If only you and I,
Get mesmerized in this night so pretty...

I don't care even if we get lost,
Like the vapors in the sky,
All that matters to me,
Is only you and I...

My heart enchants just your name,
No matter whether it's day or night,
Because in your absence,
Even with the sun there's no light...

This night will be for ours to keep,
If you hold my hand and come with me,
I'll take you places you have never seen,
You'll realize how beautiful to be loved can be...

There are no stars visible in this dark sky,
Your elegance seems to have washed them away,
Just the moon smiling at us tonight,
To lead and guide our way..

With you around I'm more me,
You give me a feeling of paradise,
Being with you is like being in a different world,
A world beyond all truths and lies...

So if only put your trust in me,
How special you are to me you'll see,
And how enchanting our togetherness can be,
If you get lost in this night with me!

- Heet N. Desai

A MIRACLE IS ALL THAT IT TAKES

Amidst a life filled with chaos,
You are a moment of peace and relief,
Truth and lies when cover this world,
You become my only hope and belief...

When the skies turn grey,
And blurriness embeds my vision,
You always stand strong by my side,
You hold my hand and show me direction...

I am sorry for the times when I made you feel low,
I was just so out of my mind,
You are just like a breeze of fresh air,
Always so gentle and kind..

You have changed my life in an amazing way,
You have no idea how much you mean to me,
But only if I could I would give you my vision,
You are so beautiful when from my eyes you see...

Your faith, love, fears and insecurities,
All in different ways I have seen,

And I promise to keep you above everything else,
Just like a king only bows in front of his queen...

Whenever you have to go away from me,
My tender heart badly aches,
But with you I feel so special and blessed,
And I realized that a miracle is all that it takes!!

- Heet N. Desai

A HAPPY MOMENT

Life is a long chain of moments,
Alternating joints of happiness and sorrows,
But those moments, which I spend with you,
Make me want to live like there's no tomorrow...

Each and every moment spent with you,
Is just impossible to put into words,
Because they make me live on the edge of life,
Give me a feeling that's still unheard...

When I hold your face between my palms,
It's like perception of paradise,
Everything around just pauses for a while,
When you put your elating charm into my eyes...

In your presence I feel like losing my senses,
Because your beauty is always raged with fire,
A fire which even the demons won't dare to touch,
Such is a moment with you, a dream, a desire...

You are so pure, so divine,
Your face would put many angels to shame,
When I am with you, in a living fairytale,
Sometimes I tend to forget my own name...

No amount of time spent with you is ever enough,
Because you make me forget my worries and fears,
Being in your arms is like being at home,
With you, in a moment, I live a thousand years!

- Heet N. Desai

YOUR HUG

Eyes are closed, and heart beats fast,
This moment I wish forever lasts,
Being in your arms is no less than the heaven,
Every single worry of mine dies...

When your arms go around my neck,
And the wall is just against my back,
When you press your face on my chest,
No words to describe, it just feels the best...

Your touch is so soothing, so warm,
Just makes everything right, nothing can go wrong,
Everything else just fades away,
The moment filled with colours, nothing left grey...

When I hold you tightly, from your waist,
Slowly and smoothly, there's no haste,
When my arms feel your gentle tenderness,
There flows a wave of inevitable happiness...

You hold me tightly, not wanting to let go,
With the shelter of sky above, and numbness of ground below,
Inside your hug is my favorite place to stay,
Without a word, a million things it says...

When I lean in forward to pull you close,
To make you feel protected, and away from chaos,
You move your face towards my neck,
Kissing me softly that very sec...

Around me when your arms are fold,
Makes me feel like I am wrapped in gold,
Gold that no money can buy,
Not on this earth, not even in the heaven up that high...

If I could, I would hug you all day and night,
Under the sun's shower and in the moon light,
Because somethings just come with good luck,
One of those is your soul touching hug!

- Heet N. Desai

FORELSKET

It comes with happiness in its hands,
To embrace you with peace, it doesn't offend,
In your eyes it leaves an everlasting spark,
In your heart it traces a beautiful mark...

It makes you meet with your own self,
In your bad times it's your sole help,
Every moment you spend in its shadow,
You'll see eternity take a bow...

It's neither harsh, nor rude,
It's strong enough to lift up your lowest mood,
And when you feel like you are all alone,
It holds you tight, places you back on the throne...

Like stars it makes your night bright,
Like sun it never keeps you out of light,
Like breeze it keeps you cool and calm,
Like a shelter it protects you from all the harm...

It takes pleasure in your lovely smile,
It stops your world, even if it is just for a while,
It stands with you against the crowd,
It makes your life turn inside out...

Believe in it, it won't ever treat you bad,
Trust in it, it will always take you ahead,
And when the angels bestow it from the heaven above,
Have faith in it; don't deny this kind of love!

- Heet N. Desai

I MET SOMEONE

I met someone in a foreign land,
So enchanting, like the dusk before the sun,
Not knowing how beautiful it would turn out to be,
Not knowing what was about to happen...

I met someone with a magical smile,
A smile that blossoms like a pretty flower,
I can sit and stare if you ask me to,
Seconds, minutes, maybe even hours...

I met someone with a charming persona,
She spreads her vibes like the waves of an ocean,
She gives my heart pre-mature ventricular systoles,
She's a perfect mixture of knowledge and emotions...

I met someone with a magnetic laughter,
Like a melody you can hear all day,
Like a rhythm that is stuck in your head,
Like your favorite song playing on replay...

I met someone with a mesmerizing voice,
Like the birds chirping early in the morning,
Didn't expect I'll meet someone here,
She came through without any warning...

I met someone who is more than just 'someone',
I still have things to say, probably a lot,
But I can't put everything on a piece of paper,
Because even a million words would fall short

- Heet N. Desai

BUTTERFLIES

Nights seem longer than usual,
Days are going by without a count,
You have made my life a season of spring,
In you something really precious I've found...

I look at you like a child looks at a merry-go-round,
With joy filled eyes and heart full of care,
You give me the feeling of butterflies in my tummy,
Making me forget all my misery and despair...

You are like a ray of hope from the sun,
Like the dawn after a dark night,
I'd never miss a chance of being with you,
Because that's the time when everything feels alright...

Why do people smile just by looking at someone?
The answer to this question I never knew...
But now I understand what they might be feeling like,
Because even in a room full of people my eyes wander to find you..

You are the best part of my day,
Without you the day seems partial and null,
You make me feel so calm and peaceful,

Like returning home after a long battle...

I'll stand up against anyone if it's for you,
Cross a fire filled ocean or climb a mountain of pain,
Not once, not twice, not ten times more,
For you I'll do it over and over again…

- Heet N. Desai

THROUGH THE DARK

When the night is long and cold,
And shivers reach right to your bone,
Remember the day isn't far away,
The day which will be our very own...

I know the things are scary right now,
But we will make it through,
Just like a rainbow forming after the rain,
Just like the fresh morning dew...

It's not always rainbows and butterflies,
Thorns are a part of the way too,
But it doesn't matter how hurting they might be,
As long as I have you..

There's a ray of light at the end of every tunnel,
A ray signifying hope and relief,
There's nothing in this world we can't get through,
If only we have our trust and belief...

Put your hand in mine,
And stars will start shinning too,
Everything will be back to colors,
Even the things which seem very blue...

Hold on for a little bit more,
Things will inevitably get better,
I know it's quite dark right now,
But the sun will surely shine later...

Sometimes it's swimming through the ocean of fire,
And sometimes it's just a walk in the park,
Just have some faith in the plan of God,
We'll fight our way through this dark!!

- Heet N. Desai

WILL YOU BE THERE?

Will you be there, when there's no one around?
Will you be, when I am feeling down?

Will you be there, when I am lost?
Will you be there, when all the doors are closed?

Will you be there, to forgive my mistakes?
Will you be there, when my hope shakes?

Will you be there, when there are thorns along the path?
Will you be there, when I am facing life's wrath?

Will you be there, when I need someone?
Will you be there, and be my shining sun?

Will you be there, to support my trembling footsteps?
Will you be there, when we go through the difficult laps?

Will you be there, when things don't fall in their place?
Will you be there, to help me get through tough days?

Will you be there, when my eyes are numb?
Will you be there, no matter what may come?

If you'll live for a hundred years,
I'll wish to live a minute less,
Because my life without you,
Would be a total mess…

- Heet N. Desai

PARADISE IS WITH YOU

Standing in the bright sunshine,
There's one thing that crosses my mind,
Although the day is so beautiful and nice,
Why doesn't it soothe my eyes?

And then I realize that you are not around,
Even the birds are chirping their melodious sound,
Cool breeze of air is complimenting it too,
But my paradise lies only with you…

You are the light when there's no sun,
You are the rainbow after the rain is done,
You are the faith when I am out of hope,
Will I ever leave you? The answer is 'nope'…

At first, I thought we would only be friends,
But little did I know we'll walk with our hand
in hand,
What love feels like, the world will see,
That you and I are forever meant to be…

You are that flower, which a bee never misses,
You are the shore an ocean wave kisses,
You are the warm beach where the sun rays lie,
With you I am always on the edge of paradise…

In every moment we spend, I live a century,
And these moments get forever preserved in my memory,
With you I am an ocean of love and bond,
But without you I am not even a small pond…

In your eyes I can see our present, future and past,
You know it's true when I say we'll forever last,
And the only thing that I want you to realize,
Is that you are so perfect when seen through my eyes…

- Heet N. Desai

SHADOWING ETERNITY

A special place just for you and me,
An inevitable bond to guide us free,
The only thing that I want you to see,
Is that we happen to shadow eternity…

It is the look in your eyes and smile on your lips,
That makes this world a better place,
With you, every moment spent is like a century,
And it's true when I say, we shadow eternity…

You make it sound so special when you take my name,
With you, I fall in love over and over again,
Your soft gentle touch mesmerizes me,
There's no doubt that we shadow eternity…

Our passion flows like the water in the ocean,
When I am with you, life moves in slow motion,
Even the moon and the stars can see,
That we are the ones shadowing eternity;
Just close your eyes and feel the breeze,
With every breeze that touches you, our love will increase,
And there's no better place where I'll rather be,
Than in your heart and in your dreams..

- Heet N. Desai

DAYDREAM REALITY

You are like the hazy sunlight in the cold winters,
Your face always as bright as the sunshine,
Your gentle breath swifts right through the autumn's call,
For me, in my life, you are an angel so divine…

The thousand fair suitors all stab at your heart,
But none too much that they can win,
Because you are like a dead person's last wish,
And you are not easy to win, I admit…

All I know is that my sun rises with you,
And the night sings a sweet song when you wish me goodnight,
And although I can't promise to defeat all your sorrows,
I'll always be with you in all your fights…

My nights which were once cold and dark,
Have now become comforting and warm,
And all my fears which once appeared so real,
Have gone far away with the storm…

Your eyes are the maze which has no way out,
Your smile so beautiful and so sweet,

Your touch so gentle and enlightening,
Just your look is enough to knock me off my feet…

Here I stand, with my hands reaching out to you,
In my heart, you own a special place,
And all I can offer, where words don't dwell,
Is a body that trembles and this love that awaits…

- Heet N. Desai

INTIMIDATING LOVE

They say love is a mistake which has no correction,
A disease which has no cure,
But baby if I have you in my arms,
I'll make the same mistake a thousand times more...

When you touch my cheeks with your cherry lips,
You take me to a world apart,
You'll realize what happens to me when I see you,
When you place your head on my beating heart...

I want to fill your life with happiness,
I want to be the reason for your smile,
And when you tell me that you love me,
My world tends to stop for a while...

All my fears tend to disappear,
When tightly my hand you hold,
And I'll love in the same way as I do today,
Even when we grow old...

Amongst the million stars in the sky,
They say heaven is there above,
But I have already found my piece of paradise,
And that is your intimidating love!

- Heet N. Desai

PROM NIGHT

In the crowd of millions,
Someone I have fond,
To tap my feet with,
Amidst the music around;
Under the dim light of the moon,
In a romantic atmosphere,
Within a plot so soft and calm,
No worries, no fears;
Stepping towards the dance floor,
With your hand in mine,
Going past the crowd,
Slowing down the pace of time;
I then pull you closer,
We begin to dance,
Ignoring the world around,
Making the fullest of this chance;
Lips are deprived of words,
But eyes break the silence of the lips,
Seems just like a fairytale,
But it is reality, stronger than any movie script;

So come with me and enjoy this beautiful night,
It will be a blast, bigger than an atom bomb,
And one question that remains standing,
Will you be my partner for prom?

\- Heet N. Desai

FEELS LIKE INFINITY…

Every night when I look up in the sky,
Amongst the million stars, till the very end,
With the heaven above and earth below,
I see your face again and again…

The number of nights it takes to count the stars,
Till the very last one at that height above,
Is the time I'll be by your side,
Is the time till I'll give you all my love…

I can feel your heart beating in mine,
And your eyes, without any doubt, own me,
I always feel alive when I spend my time with you,
Because your love is the only thing that sets me free…

Up in the sky when you'll look at the clouds,
I'll be there appearing very sober,
Just waiting for you to come up here,
So that we both can be much closer

They say love is a great thing,
And that greater thing doesn't exist,
If that is true,
Then this feeling is something I just cannot resist…

I was born to make you mine,
And you were born for mine to be,
Yes I am selfish, because I want you all to me,
And with you, time always feels like infinity!!

- Heet N. Desai

DISTANCE IS JUST A NUMBER

Seven billion people around the globe,
But someday, somewhere I had to meet her,
The day was bright, the sky was blue,
The first time when I saw her…

Her voice was like a Nightingale's song,
The spark in her eyes put the stars to shame,
'Hi, it's a pleasure to meet you', I said,
Reciprocating, she told me her name…

Things were fine and smooth between us,
Our relation headed in a new direction,
Little did I know how beautiful it would be,
How happily we would reach new levels of perfection…

When I met her for the first time,
I saw her as a mesmerizing angel,
But if you ask me to describe her beauty in words,
All I'll be able to say is that she's more of an archangel…

And now that I have to leave from here,
My heart aches that I won't be able to see her for long,

But even if the distance tends to keep us apart,
She is the one to whom my heart will always belong…

Even if I have to leave now,
The distance doesn't matter to the hearts that care,
For the moments and memories always span the miles,
And within a few seconds, with each other, we are back there…

- Heet N. Desai

DREAM COME TRUE

In the fast moving life filled with noise and chaos,
It's quite difficult for happiness and sorrows to part,
But since the time I have known you,
There's a new reason of happiness for my heart…

Dreams, wishes, prayers, all seem to have come true,
There's nothing more left to ask for,
You have no idea how special you are to me,
You mean the world to me and much more…

The story of my life took a turn,
With you, everything feels like a fairytale,
My heart started flying like a free bird,
Which was once locked in its own jail..

Suddenly all the love songs started making sense,
Each line of them reminded me of you,
And now every time that we are together,
Cool breeze blows and skies turn blue…

I love you for all that you have been,
For all that you are and all that you are yet to be,
You'll realize how beautiful you are,
If only from my eyes you see…

You are so cute even when you try not to be,
Your eyes speak a million words even when you are silent,
You carry a vibe so pure and divine,
And your approach is always so vibrant..

No matter which ever place I visit,
My favorite spot will be right next to you,
I cross my heart and swear to you,
That your presence in my life is just like a dream come true…

- Heet N. Desai

BEAUTIFUL YOU!

You are the like the melody of a song,
More beautiful than any of the flowers,
Loving and caring, just like a fairy,
Prettier than any of the stars..

I'll walk with you through storms and thorns,
Even if it is a million miles,
And I promise that no matter what,
Your lips won't ever be devoid of that smile…

When you look at me with those lovely eyes,
I just wish to get lost in them forever,
And will I ever want to come out?
The answer is 'never'…

Your beauty won't fade away with age,
Nor will your charm and glamour dim,
Because they aren't just superficial things,
They come from the heart within…

You have a golden heart,
There's not a second thought about it,
And with the threads of your faith and hope,
My dreams I want to knit…

Every moment spent with you,
Is like waking on fresh morning dew,
And I thank God every day,
To bring me across a woman as amazing as you..

- Heet N. Desai

SHE CARES LIKE AN ANGEL

Enveloped in darkness was my tender heart,
No light to direct the way,
Far from rays of hope and courage,
Waiting to escape this night and enter a new day…

Although there was silence scattered all around,
My mind was always occupied with chaos,
And although everything seems so normal,
Life was to be on the edge of havoc…

This darkness and chaos started killing me slowly,
Poisoning me a little each day,
There was no one to share my sorrows with,
No one to whom all these things I could say…

But as they say, hope is the last thing to lose,
You never know what tomorrow will bring,
I kept holding on tight,
Hoping that someday my fate will ring…

And one fine day, she came into my life,
From heaven above, to destroy my troubles and fears,
Although she was a stranger to me,
She felt someone to be very close and dear…

She understood me better than anyone else,
She was more caring than I could ever be,
She became my hope and reason to live,
This thing very clearly I could see…

She loved me enough to make me forget my miseries,
Her touch always felt so warm and fine,
She set the strings of my life back into tune,
To produce the most melodious hymn…

So now peace and happiness dwells in my heart,
Where once chaos and sorrows were paired,
I broke the shackles of darkness, reaching out to light,
All because an angel cared!

- Heet N. Desai

THE FAREWELL

Time for us to say goodbye,
Time for me to show some sorrowful sighs;
Following your dreams you are taking off today,
Ready to encounter new challenges in your way;
A young bird is all set to fly,
Reaching out to success on the cloud so high;
You are going miles away, over seven seas,
That is the only vision my eyes can see;
Maybe with times, with difficulties you'll have to cope,
But remember, nothing is impossible once you chose hope;
You have grabbed a golden chance in this competitive universe,
Your talent can't be described even in a million verses;
This chance is a bull's eyes that you have hit,
Make sure to make the best of it;
You'll be in new surroundings; you'll find new friends,
You'll meet new people; you'll shake new hands;
You'll have a new platform to show your capabilities,
You'll have the opportunity to explore new cities…

Amidst all the charm, happiness and glee,
Please take care that you don't forget me;
Just one thing that I want you to see,
For you, till my last breath, I'll always be…

- Heet N. Desai

CONNECTION

The other night, I saw a girl,
Looking so pretty, in her own twirl,
My eyes were just stuck for a while,
When she displayed her enchanting smile…

I have no idea who she is,
With looks as sparkling as appy fizz,
In the night so dark where everything was blur,
I just couldn't get my eyes off her…

It was like butterflies flying in my gut,
And there was no way for them to shut,
Because the way she danced was just so mesmerizing,
Just like after a long night you see the sun rising…

It's not something you feel every day,
Nor is it something to everyone you say,
But that night I felt something special inside,
Something from which I didn't want to hide…

If I ever see that beautiful face again,
No matter whichever place, a club or a lane,
I'll walk upto her and put my words into action,
To let her know that with her I felt an undeniable
connection…

\- Heet N. Desai

IT'S NOT ALWAYS RAINBOWS AND BUTTERFLIES

• • •

NO ONE TO LISTEN

Amidst the clouds of memory,
And beneath the mighty bright sun,
I want to speak my heart out,
But there's no one listen…

All my failures and triumphs,
Everything that I lost and earned,
All these moments I want to share,
But there's no one to listen…

The feeling of love scattered in my heart,
And the feelings that hurt and burn,
All these feelings I want to share,
But there's no one to listen…

The ocean of thoughts roaring in my head,
And the storms of emotions that make me twist and turn,
This state of mind I want to convey,
But there's no one to listen…

The journey of my life so far,
All the difficulties I face and things I learnt,
All those things I want to narrate,
But there's no one to listen…

The words spoken by my silence,
And the valley of silence in which I run,
All these things I want to talk about,
But there's no one to listen…

- Heet N. Desai

A LITTLE TOO LATE

Here I am, standing in front of this wall,
With millions of thoughts running through my mind,
No whispers, no murmurs, silence is all around,
Seems like all the memories are getting rewind..

She is there on the other side of this wall,
So quiet, just like a silent lake,
There are so many things that she wants to say,
But she is hiding all her sorrows behind the smile that she fakes..

If only she tells me , I'll break the wall and get through it,
And then hold her tight in my arms,
But she is standing there just like a shadow,
And now I'm longing for her and her charms..

I don't know what is she afraid of?
What is stopping her from talking to me?
Maybe she has her own reasons,
But I don't think this is how it's meant to be..

By this time I lose all my patience,
So I try to break the wall and get on the other side,

And finally when I succeed in doing that,
What I see there is just like a dark night..

She was lying there on the ground, pale & white,
Just like a fallen dead leaf,
I run to her and take her in my arms,
And I try to wake her up with my heart filled with grief..

I call her name a million times,
In a hope that she may listen to me,
But all I hear is this frightful silence,
And I just feel like a person stuck in the middle of the sea..

She was DEAD, she had gone forever,
I broke into tears,
The world seemed to have fallen down for me,
I could still hear her voice ringing in my ears..

I noticed she had gripped something in her fist,
It was a note for me, I unfolded it with sorrow,
My heart was shaking when I was unfolding it,
And the note read as follows:
"I'm taking the last few breaths of my life,
And soon I'll leave this mortal world forever,

But promise me you'll be happy by cherishing the moments we shared,
And for me, you'll cry never..
I love you a lot and I'll always do,
And I'll never go apart,
And no matter even if I'm not in this world,
I'll always stay with you in your heart.."

She wants me to be happy, and if that's her last wish,
I'll try my best to do it for her,
And even if she'll stay quiet for the rest of my life,
Her voice will always be safe in my heart as delightful murmurs..

Maybe I took a lot of time to break that wall,
Maybe I could have met her for the one last time,
But now she is present only in my memories,
And she'll be alive within me throughout my lifetime..

- Heet N. Desai

CROSSROADS: PARTING

There is this girl so simple and sweet,
She loves to be in her own world of imagination,
I love the way she talks and laughs,
And in times of need she has been my motivation..

Every single day of mine is incomplete without her,
Her looks, her eyes, her voice, her touch,
Whenever she is not around,
All these things I miss so much..

But this has become yesterday,
And it is just a memory,
The clouds have started to gather now,
And the leaves are falling from the tree..

Tears come to my eyes when I think of her,
A cute smile was always displayed on her face,
I remember the times when our friendship was new,
And I felt she was the only one I wanted to amaze..

But now the things are not the way they used to be,
And I guess there's no one who deserves the blame,
She has decided to take another path,
While I am still walking on the same..

And now I have this feeling of feeling nothing at all,
I am walled off emotions, unconscious with dreams of bliss,
Frantically grasping for a hold,
And being dragged further into an abyss..

I just want her to take the burden off her shoulders,
For the paths we are talking about are far apart,
It seems like she has already decided to travel the new road,
So I think even I need to depart..

I don't know how the things between us got ruined,
I don't know who created this division in our road,
But it is how it is right now,
And it feels like rains of sorrows are being heavily poured..

So here I am saying the final goodbye,
As much as I know, we can't stay,
Spending one last minute lost in her eyes,
Hoping that our roads will cross again some other day..

- Heet N. Desai

WHEN AN ANGEL CRIES

I had a dream; I was on my knees,
On the top of a hill,
Looking at the vast clear blue sky,
And everything around appeared so still.

The wind was blowing like never before,
And the leaves were saying goodbye to the trees,
No one was with me in this scenario,
Only my mind carrying a few memories..

I tried to cry to relieve my grief,
But there was no one around to comfort,
Although it was burning inside,
I couldn't describe how intense was the hurt.

There were shouts from my mouth,
But my lips were deprived of all the words,
The wind was racing my voice away,
My own screams couldn't be heard.

Raising my fists I asked heaven,
"Please show some mercy on me.",
But there was nothing that I could hear in return,
And silence was the only reply to my plea.

Moments later I heard a faint melody,
It was the choir of Angels singing from above,
And then the great God gave his words from heaven,
"This world is reaping hatred, because it isn't sowing love."

When the angels concluded their final carol,
A shower of rain sparkled, but without any cloud in the sky,
I was confused, how can this happen?
God then whispered, "This is how an Angel cries."

- Heet N. Desai

SEPARATION

I close my eyes and I see you here,
I try to touch you, but you disappear,
I open my eyes with a sigh of grief,
Crying for just a moment of relief…

I wish I hadn't let you out of that door,
And now I think we could have been so much more,
But maybe our fate had already rung the alarm,
And now you are in my heart but not in my arms…

When you were with me life was just like a paradise,
And now it seems worse than hell,
Once a beautiful spring has now become an euphoric winter,
And even this world seems to be a prison's cell…

I still remember the first time we met,
I was so nervous to talk to you,
Your enslaving beauty had left me out of words,
It felt like there is no one else in this world, just us two…

Till today those times make me nostalgic,
They make my tender heart so numb,
And my heart is so tired and exhausted now,

It says it doesn't want to pump…

There you are going away from me,
Going away with our memories too,
To a new place, to start a new life,
But remember, someone here is living just for you…

- Heet N. Desai

ESCAPE

Shouts, screams, laughter, cries,
Talks, fights, truths and lies,
It's really becoming tough to survive,
I am tired of leading this monotonous life…

Same places to visit every day,
Same people to meet and same things to say,
Embracing the same mornings and nights,
Same routine and schedule so tight…

I just want to leave everything and escape,
Somewhere I can mold my life in my desired shape,
Where I can feel the wind beneath my feet,
Where I can hear my own heart beat…

I want to escape in search of solace,
The place where I can create my own little space,
Where there are no city lights and crowds,
Where the fields are green and the sky is free of clouds…

I want to deceive this artificial life,
Because it seems like walking on the edge of a knife,
I want to go to a place where my silence can be heard,
I want to go there where I can fly free like a bird…

I want to find that place where miracles originate,
Where life is independent of destiny and fate,
Where there will be no one else but me,
Such a place I wish to see…

I hope to succeed in my search one day,
In the green meadows, amidst the nature, where my life I can reshape,
Where my thoughts and visions can be saved,
That is the place where I'll escape…

- Heet N. Desai

LONELINESS

The surroundings have become quieter,
And my heart whispers it wants some rest,
Even my shadow has left me alone,
And I am in my brain's arrest..

I try to figure out what is darker,
The darkness outside or inside me,
The only answer that reaches my ears,
Is that from this darkness I cannot get free..

Even the stars aren't showing their shine tonight,
And the moon is hidden behind that dark cloud,
There's only emptiness around me,
So it doesn't matter how loud I shout..

The street where once there was a merry crowd of people,
Now it only comprises of memories,
People, relations, time and life,
Everything has changed in quick successive series..

In which direction should I go? I have no clue,
Because it's dark everywhere and I can't see anyone else wandering,
The night is getting even darker,

So I decide to just sit here and wait for the morning…

Seems like even the sun has lost its way,
Because it's been such a long night and still there isn't any ray of light,
So I just close my eyes and try to calm myself,
Waiting for the end of this dreadful night..

I know that soon this darkness will be killed by a new sunrise,
And life will clear out this emptiness,
But for now the only thing in my sight,
Is this darkness filled with loneliness..

- Heet N. Desai

YES, I LOVED HER

Among the thousand voices in my head,
There was a voice which used to reach my heart,
The voice as sweet as a melodious song,
But now that voice is just off the chart...

That voice was of my other half,
The girl whom I loved more than myself,
In her eyes I found my way to heaven,
But the steps of that way she broke by herself...

In the beautiful nights gone by,
I always used to see her while I was asleep,
But now when she comes in my dreams my nights are troubled,
Because now my heart is too numb to weep..

I can't deny that I loved her,
But now I don't even wish to see her again,
The street in which we used to walk hand in hand,
Has now become just a lonely lane...

Every moment we spent together was just an illusion,
And I was mistaken to believe it as the truth,
The only truth that always prevailed,

Was that someday she was going to change her
route..

It grieves me to think that she manipulated my heart,
And she left without giving any proper reason,
This showed me how fast she changes her colors,
Just like a year of changing seasons…

If only my heart could see what was visible to my
eyes,
I could have prevented these rolling tears,
But now I don't want to regret anything,
And I want to change this sorrowful atmosphere…

So the story ends on the note that I once loved her,
And this fact I cannot change,
But now I have to get over her and her memories,
And I am strong enough to accept this challenge…

- Heet N. Desai

THE REALMS OF OUR PAST

Last night as I was lying on my bed,
Thoughts of our past were running through my head,
Those magical days when everything was perfect,
We were strongly bonded by our love pact...

Remember the first time we hugged each other,
Like nothing else in this world matters,
Only the two of us in this world so bright,
Feeling each other's heart beats in that beautiful night...

Those late night chats which we wished never ended,
Those little secrets, from each other that we defended,
Teasing each other with various names,
Playing those cliché rapid fire games...

There's no doubt that we also fought,
But we only fight with those, whom we love a lot,
Those fights also brought us closer,
Helped us in understanding each other...

Where has all of it disappeared now?
Where did it vanish that we once called love?
I could have never imagined not talking to you,
So why is it happening now? I have no clue...

I want the old us back together,
So that we can make our situations better,
Flourishing again with the same affection and care,
Because I can't afford losing a person like you, so rare..

So will you please give me my old girl back?
I promise I'll protect you from all the emotional attack,
I assure you that forever we'll last,
If only we can live again in the realms of our past…

- Heet N. Desai

CROSSROADS: Part 2

Never thought that this moment would come so soon,
When I'll have to bid you farewell,
Your presence in my life was something so special,
With you by my side I could have even accepted hell...

But now you are standing there,
On the other side of this airport gate,
With few tears and ambitions in your eyes,
Well, I guess this is the decision of our fate...

How I wish that the time paused in this very moment,
So that I can forever remain lost in your eyes,
I am happy that you are embracing a new chapter,
But what hurts is this inevitable goodbye...

I have never imagined my life without you in it,
And now that you are going I don't know how I am going to be,
The moment you gave me that Mississippi long hug,
I felt no one is in this world, just you and me...

Your every step towards boarding your flight,
Makes me lose my control over tears,
Although a smile is displayed on my face,

This moment I would have given anything to keep you near…

I remember you telling me that I get too emotional at times,
But this time I can see your eyes filled with the same emotions,
You are leaving this shore and heading for the other one,
Over seven seas, crossing four oceans…

No words can express how much I'll miss you,
Because you have always been the half that completed me,
There was absolutely nothing that I couldn't share with you,
Because you always possessed my heart's key…

A million memories we have created for ourselves,
I'll keep all of them secured in my heart,
Even though the distance keeps us away,
I am sure we'll never be emotionally apart…

So when our roads cross again someday,
The same laughter and memories in our way will lie,
Again the same emotions will fill our hearts,
With a smile on our faces and tears in our eyes…

\- Heet N. Desai

HOPE

IS

THE

LAST

THING

TO

LOSE

...

AGAINST THE ODDS

Life at times is so unpredictable,
Just like an atom which can be unstable..
Sometimes it's good and sometimes bad,
But no matter what, it always takes us ahead..

It is a journey where we are the travellers,
It is a ship and we are the sailors..
It can make us the most evolved species,
But in no time it can also break us into pieces..

It makes us face many difficulties,
But it also provides us with many faculties..
We are placed in situations where we feel we are lost,
But we need to rise from there at any cost..

Look at life positively and you'll become bolder,
Because beauty lies in the eyes of the beholder..
Challenges will always come in your way,
But learn not to turn your face away..

Think differently, and solve every problem bit by bit,
Because a problem cannot be solved with the same
mind that created it..
However big a problem is, go through its every lap,

Because a journey of a thousand miles begins with a single step..

Chase your dreams and you'll admit,
That if you can dream it, you can achieve it..
Don't worry if no one stands with you,
Because you yourself are enough to explore something new..

Even if people around you don't care,
Always remember, even the plane takes off against the air..

\- Heet N. Desai

WHEN YOUR PAST CALLS

Breaking the shackles of time,
And swimming through the ocean of fate,
I brought myself in the future,
Ignoring every pain and hate..

I left behind the things,
Those once filled my empty heart,
Thinking some miracle was waiting for me,
And my life was ready to create its own art..

But what happens when that previous time comes in front of you,
And you realize that the ocean you swam was a circle,
You come back to the point you thought you would never be at,
And you become the part of an unwanted cycle..

Now here I stand, right in front of my past,
Thinking how to react,
Whether to answer it and repeat the cycle,
Or just move without undertaking any act..

Thinking for a long time I finally chose the second option,
Because my past had nothing new to say,

So rather than wasting my time on it,
I should walk towards my future keeping the past away..

I find it a little tough to ignore my past and just walk away,
But I guess that is how it is supposed to be,
Because past is something which cannot be changed,
And I don't want to move with its burden on me..

Without wasting any more time,
And making firm my mind,
I decide to cross the tunnel of fortune,
Leaving my past behind..

So facing this reality I realized..

When you sense loneliness developing in your heart,
And you find yourself surrounded by time's wall,
When your life seems to drag you back,
It all happens when your past calls..

- Heet N. Desai

BELIEVE AND THE WORLD IS YOURS

Life is a box full of opportunities,
And you can't afford to miss even a single one,
Only with trust and faith in oneself,
The whole world and everything in it can be won..

The day you are born, a new era begins,
An era in which you are the Queen/King,
If you wish, you can dominate this world,
And soar high like an eagle with your dreams on your wings..

The span between your birth and death,
Is completely in your hands,
It depends on you what you make out of it,
Become a slave or the Prince/Princess of this land..

Life won't be a bed of roses,
You will come across hurdles in your way,
But only if you have that fire in you,
You surely can overcome those hurdles, no matter what people say..

So take the oath of believing in you,
And you'll become bolder for sure,

Because 'Belief' is the thing which will lead you to success,

Just believe, and the world will be yours..

- Heet N. Desai

WALKING IN THE LIGHT OF HOPE

I am walking in the light of hope,
With some dreams in my eyes,
Heading towards the shore of success,
With no laughter or cries..

My passion of dreams guides my way,
I walk the path of thorns,
And cross the valley of destiny,
Which seemed completely shattered and torn..

At times I feel I can't go on,
But that light of hope never fades,
It encourages me to keep pushing on,
Saying that its only hard-work with which histories are made,

So I get up and start moving again,
With the same passion in my heart,
Until I achieve my goals and aims,
And my dreams and reality can never part..

As I move closer towards my dreams,
The light of hope gets brighter,

I find myself nearer to my goal,
And I hold on my passion of dreams tighter..

I am still on my journey and I have learnt,
That there's nothing with which you can't cope,
Be strong enough to carry your dreams with you,
And walk in the light of hope..

- Heet N. Desai

THE STRANGER ME

As I wake everyday with the breaking of my alarm,
And stand in front of the mirror,
I see a stranger's face in it,
And rolling down his cheek is a round big tear,

I move closer to have a clearer vision,
And try to figure out his identity,
And soon I realize that the stranger in the mirror,
Was no one else but me..

I was still in a perplexed state of mind,
Could that person really be me?
Because I was never this way the mirror showed,
And this wasn't the image that I used to see..

I had lost myself somewhere in the mysterious hours,
And my identity was hidden behind that stranger's face,
I am confuse how to bring back myself,
And I don't know this will enslave me for how many more days..

I have puzzled myself with all sorts of questions and doubts,
And now I have to resolve this mystery,

Because I find no other way to break the shackles of this stranger's face,
And now I just feel like a bird which cannot fly free..

But I still have a ray of hope inside me,
And I think that's enough to get me back,
I believe that once again I'll be the real me,
And I'll stand firm on the sailing ship's deck..

So now is the time to face that stranger,
And I am not sure if it will be my loss or gain,
But I believe I am strong enough to defeat that stranger,
And I'll meet myself once again..

- Heet N. Desai

EVERY PROBLEM IS AN OPPORTUNITY

Every problem is an opportunity if you know how to grab it,
Every question comes with an answer if you know how to trap it,
It's just the difference of perspective which turns a problem into solution,
And it is this perspective which creates an all new vision..

The hurdles of life you face,
And when you get lost in the problem's maze,
Remember that you carry the potential to deal with it,
And when you realize that, the candles of hope are lit..

If you feel something is suppressing you,
And the ways of getting out of it are very few,
Try to face it with a different view,
And you'll realize that its solution is hidden inside of you..

Every problem you solve gives you the courage to solve another one,
Then you start dominating over your problems and see how the tables turn,

You need to see that another door of solution opens when one closes,
And you need to be strong because life won't always be a bed of roses..

So if any problem challenges your power or dignity,
Remember that this problem is an opportunity,
An opportunity to show that you are capable of tackling it,
And to prove that if the problem is hard, you are harder enough to hit it..

Always keep your head high,
And then see how the problems die,
So promise yourself that you will become bolder,
Because God gives his toughest battles to His strongest soldiers..

\- Heet N. Desai

SURFING ON THE WAVE OF LIFE

The road to success is not a straight path,
We need to move with patience and not wrath..
At every mile of this road life shows us a different scene,
We meet failures at times and at times we also win..

These triumphs and failures are just like a wave in the sea,
Sometimes we are on the top of this wave and sometimes we are down on our knees..
But let neither happiness nor sorrows in any way affect you,
Let neither of them get over your head or make you feel blue..

Live the life the way you want to,
As God has bestowed this life as a gift upon you..
At times you'll find things are not falling in their place,
And problems and puzzles are almost being thrown at your face..

But that doesn't mean you are not capable of handling it,
Here, God is just testing your patience and wit..

No matter what the situation is, if you are in a group or alone,

Just carry your will power with you and keep moving on..

Dare to take the risk of going far away,

And you'll notice opportunities lying in your way..

Always believe that nothing is impossible,

Because once you chose hope anything is possible..

This is the wave of life which makes you surf more and more,

And people who learn to surf on it are sure to reach their shore..

\- Heet N. Desai

THE SUN WILL RISE AGAIN

Alone we sit, with the darkness dwelling in us,
Cursing our sorrows and pain,
Complaining to God about the problems we face,
And asking Him what have we gained...

We feel we are the only one facing all the dilemmas of life,
And that we are being attacked by our griefs,
Rather than fighting back we surrender to our quandaries,
And then we start feeling like dead autumn leaves...

But understand, just like there's no lock without a key,
There can never be a problem which has no solution,
And unless we learn to bounce back from circumstances,
There is no way we can create a revolution...

People around us are fighting their own battles,
Maybe they are dealing with problems bigger than what we face,
So before cursing our sorrows we must realize,
That in life there'll always be a good and bad phase...

We need to treat both the phases with a smile,
And not let them affect us to a large extent,
Just hold on, be strong, situation gets better,
It's life and we have to learn to comprehend…

So grapple your troubles, fight out your misery,
And I assure you your efforts won't go in vain,
Although the sun is below the horizon today,
Tomorrow it will rise again…

\- Heet N. Desai

LET'S FACE THE FEARS

You are not afraid of the storm,
You are afraid of its disaster,
You are not afraid of the jump,
You are afraid of falling faster…

You are not afraid of the fire,
You are afraid of getting burnt,
You are not afraid of acting stupid,
You are afraid of losing the respect you have earned…

You are not afraid of the darkness,
You are afraid of what's in it,
You are not afraid of fighting your misery,
You are afraid of being hit…

You are not afraid of the heights,
You are afraid of the fall,
You are not afraid of speaking the truth,
You are afraid of answering it to all…

You are not afraid of giving an exam,
You are afraid of its result,
You are not afraid of taking someone's side,
You are afraid of its insult…

You are not afraid of the water,
You are afraid of the drown,
You are not afraid of climbing high,
You are afraid of looking down…

You are not afraid of answering a question,
You are afraid of answering it wrong,
You are not afraid of commitment,
You are afraid of not obeying it for long…

You are not afraid of facing your fears,
You are afraid of trying,
You are not afraid of risking your life,
You are afraid of dying…

So let's face all our fears today,
Let's punch them all on their faces,
Let's defeat them in the court of life,
And let's be the judge of our own cases…

- Heet N. Desai

IT'S OKAY

It's okay if you have cried today,
Tomorrow you'll laugh,
It's okay if you have problems today,
Tomorrow they'll become half..

It's okay if your day was bad today,
Tomorrow it will be fresh and new,
It's okay if your parents yelled today,
Tomorrow they'll stand with you..

It's okay if you have failed your exam today,
Tomorrow you'll be among the toppers,
It's okay if you have no job today,
Tomorrow you'll earn in dollars..

It's okay if you have no friends today,
Tomorrow your popularity will speak,
It's okay if your talents aren't valued today,
Tomorrow they'll be rated as unique..

It's okay if your partner left you today,
Tomorrow you'll find someone better,
It's okay if you have sorrows today,
Tomorrow they'll shatter..

It's okay if you are broken today,
Tomorrow you'll come back stronger,
It's okay if you can't walk a short distance today,
Tomorrow you'll run distances even longer..

It's okay if you fought with your best friend today,
Tomorrow this fight will mold into love,
It's okay if you are at the bottom of success today,
Tomorrow you'll be much above..

Remember it's not a bad life,
It might just be a bad day,
And also remember to remind yourself,
Sometimes, it's okay not to be okay!

- Heet N. Desai

FACE A CHALLENGE HEAD TO HEAD

'I cannot do it.'
'There's no hope left.'
'It is way out of my reach.'
'It's just impossible.'

Do we use these statements when the problems are challenging?
Or when we think that by our efforts they won't be changing?
But the foremost thing in facing any problem,
Is to know that you are capable of sending it back from where it came…

No matter how ever big is challenge is,
You must carry the attitude of fighting it…
Just because of the fear of loss you cannot give up on trying,
What is the worst that can happen? You'll end up lost and crying…

So what? At least you'll have the satisfaction that you tried,
That you were capable of answering it when it was on your opposite side…

Strength isn't shown when the situation is easy,
It is shown when you are down and things aren't breezy…

Strength is shown when the situation laughs at you,
When the ways of getting out of it are very few…
Don't have the panic of facing failures,
You'll meet the everyday, every week, every month, every year…

Remember, storms help the trees to find their roots deeper,
And when we smile at our problems, their values become cheaper…
Just like the two sides of a coin,
Where there are clouds of grieves, the bright sunlight of happiness will also join…

- Heet N. Desai

HOLD YOUR HEAD HIGH

Packed with a million surprises life is a gift,
From happiness to grief and back it makes the shift,
And people who learn to deal with all the circumstances,
Are the ones who aren't bounded by limits or fences…

We normally tend to give up when something doesn't work out,
Creating negativity, generating vague doubt,
If things don't work out change your plan as a whole,
But don't ever think about giving up on your goal…

An old end will always lead to a new beginning,
If you didn't play well in this one, there'll be another inning,
Life is hard, but it's also beautiful,
Sometimes it's grey, but it also turns colorful…

Take chances, take risks, and hold your head high,
You need to deal with the dust before you can touch the sky,
Because in the end we only regret the chances we didn't take,
To fulfill our dreams from our sleep we'll need to wake…

There won't be success without failures and falls,
You need to answer back when a challenge calls,
Your problems and failures won't end overnight,
But you can crush them for sure if only you decide to fight…

- Heet N. Desai

FALL SEVEN TIMES STAND UP EIGHT

In life, two situations are never the same,
Nor are the intensities of two circumstances,
But you won't know how strong you are,
Until you decide to take your chances...

Even if you fail over and over again,
Every time you'll learn something new,
Because unless the thing doesn't challenge you,
It will never change you...

You have got to believe in yourself,
No matter if others do it or not,
Because they aren't in your shoes to know how you feel,
And you'll tell them how bravely you have fought...

Never hesitate to make mistakes,
Because life begins once you are out of your comfort zone,
And no one will tell you when to do that,
'You'll have' to take that decision by your own...

It's never about being the best,
It's about being better than you were yesterday,

And once this thing gets lodged in your mind,
You are sure to find your own way...

You'll never know what's behind that wall,
Unless you have the courage to open the gate,
You'll succeed one day if you keep on trying,
Fall seven times, stand up eight...

- Heet N. Desai

FOR THE COUNTRY

• • •

DIVE INTO DIVERSITY

The land of cultures and religions,
Where more than a hundred languages are spoken,
A country which is the biggest democracy,
And where the shackles of tourism are broken…

From north to south and east to west,
Unbounded places to explore,
And sceneries so fascinating and breathtaking,
That you cannot ask for anything more…

Kashmir, known as 'The Paradise on Earth',
Crowns our beautiful motherland,
A country blessed with everything,
Wildlife, mountains, rivers and sand…

Where souls like Aryabhatta were born,
Where leaders like Subhash Chandra Bose prevailed,
Where people of diversified castes and creed thrive together,
And united they share their happiness and pain…

A country bordered by the Great Himalayas,
Where the Mt. Everest stands firm and high,
A country possessing a huge network of rivers,
That forms a beautiful tangle tie…

Where the winds of deserts in the west,
Are intercepted by the Bay of Bengal in the east,
Where the roars of majestic mountains,
Are heard in valleys enveloped in fog and mist…

These are merely any points about this vast land,
And you are still left to be taken to its core,
So move out of your houses to witness fantabulous India,
And start exploring more…

- Heet N. Desai

I AM COMING BACK HOME

Standing with a gun on this border,
With my pockets filled with bullets and bombs,
I live like a shadow here,
With a heart and soul always so numb..

My dreams tell me to go back home,
Where I can stay close to my dear ones,
But my eyes cannot ignore my country's flag,
Because I am a soldier standing on this border with a gun…

Bullets hit every part of my body,
But they cannot touch my courage and strength,
I'll fight for my country till my breath supports,
Even if I see my death standing at an arm's length…

Every war I fight I think it to be my last,
Because I don't know when my fate will leave my side,
And when I sleep at night after killing hundreds of people,
My heart silently weeps which my eyes try to hide…

Although these people are of opposite army,
They too have friends and families,
But we soldiers are trained to be emotionless,
And we need to do our job, whether happily or unhappily...

The always so bright sun was about to set,
Maybe it doesn't wish to witness tonight's war,
The war which will make the sky grey again,
The war which will kill thousands or more...

Just before the war I read a letter from my family,
It said "Come home soon."
My tear filled eyes made the words appear blur,
The sun was down the horizon, came out the moon...

Firing started, missiles were launched,
The smoke began to spread all over,
This time the bullet hit right on my chest,
And my heart rate started to get slower...

Finally when the war ended,
My body was sleeping in the lap of my motherland,
Although my heart had stopped beating,
A smile was on my face with my country's flag in my hand...

My body was taken back to my native land,
Where it was covered with a tricolor flag,
Rifles were fired in my honor,
And to the great God I was going back…

Although I won't be able to serve my country anymore,
I'm happy that I was being fare welled from my native place,
The place where I was born and brought up,
That's where I ended my life's case…

- Heet N. Desai

MISCELLANEOUS

• • •

JOURNEY FROM NIGHT TO DAY

Working all day long,
As I lay on bed at night,
The stars peeping from the sky above,
Seem to hold me so tight..

This night carries some magic with it,
Hypnotizing me with its beauty,
And no wonder I am lost in it,
Forgetting all my chores and duty..

Then begins the journey in the land of dreams,
Where the only prevailing thing is peace,
The only existing season is Spring,
And where life moves with such an ease..

This journey ends with the breaking dawn,
And I wake with the sun rays falling on my face,
Hearing the birds chirp in this fresh morning,
And the new sunrise, with my very eyes I gaze..

This sunrise brings with it a positive vibration,
And I get off my bed with new goals in my way,
New dreams to chase and new promises to make,
Starting with positive vibes a brand new day..

The time between glowing stars and the rising sun,
Whispered the things it had to say,
And I was quietly listening to it,
As I was on my journey from night to day..

- Heet N. Desai

THOSE SHOOTING STARS

As the tired sun sets at the end of the day,
The moon comes over to take its place,
But it isn't alone in this lovely night sky,
The twinkling stars also occupy their respective space...

Come lie down with me on this wet grass,
Listen to what the moon and stars have to say,
Enjoy the delightful sight of the dancing sky,
Before this view gets stolen by the sun's rays...

As my eyes jump from one star to another,
I catch some of the loveliest sights,
The sight of puzzled constellations,
Formed so beautifully at such an height...

Suddenly I notice something jumping from the sky,
And that view was something more than great,
Streaks of bright light across the dark sky,
That was something my heart would happily take...

They were the shooting stars as we call them,
Decorating the enchanting night,
Complimenting it was the wet grass beneath me,
And the atmosphere so cool and quiet...

Shooting stars aren't the stars in real,
But the burnt meteorites thrown from the outer space,
It doesn't matter if they are stars or meteorites,
As long as they bring a smile on my face..

So here I am on this wet grass,
Watching those shooting stars passing over my head,
But as the first rays of morning break the magic of night,
I find myself waking on my bed…

- Heet N. Desai

THE INEVITABLE TRUTH

Our journey begins from the time we are born,
And continues till eternity,
So every moment we live is a gift,
And then comes to our door the inevitable mortality...

But I feel that this whole life is an illusion,
And Death is the only truth,
Because life comes with no guarantee,
But Death comes for sure, whether kind or rude...

This world is a place of immortals,
As each and every soul here will take an exit someday,
The life after death is what will remain forever,
But what is the life after death? No one can say...

Life can be fair or unfair to us,
But we all are equal in Death's eyes,
Maybe we can succeed in cheating our lives,
But nothing works in front of Death, no truths, no lies...

Each day we spend we are brought closer to our Death,
Or maybe the Death starts coming closer and closer,

And when we complete our role in the drama called life,
Death arrives to tell us that our time on this earth is over...

So use your wisdom and make the best of your lives,
In this rush don't forget your way,
Take everything that you can from life,
Because when life starts taking back, it even takes your breath away…

- Heet N. Desai

I LEARNT TO LIVE THAT NIGHT

Struggles, success, rise, falls,
Life is full of such imposters,
Sometimes we laugh, sometimes we cry,
Sometimes life's a boon, but sometimes it's also a curse...

Standing on the ground we want to touch the sky,
And the distance between the two is the journey we call success,
In our way we'll have to face many challenges,
Sometimes even with ourselves we'll have to clash...

That night when I was lying on my bed,
A voice from my heart silently said,

"The pain you carry is for what reasons?
In life, happiness and sorrows are two seasons,
None of them remains for too long,
They are like the two sides of a coin, to everyone they belong;
Life is a roller-coaster of emotions,
It is like a mixture of four oceans;
Get up, chase your dreams,
Before your voice turns into screams;
There's always going to be something in your way,

People will have a lot of things to say;
But you know you got to believe in yourself,
You have to be your own help;
So now stop crying and wipe off the tears,
You have to touch the sky, leaving behind your fears."

That night I learnt some lessons of life,
The overpowered darkness had some moonlight I believe,
Maybe it took me a little more time,
But that night I finally learnt to live!

- Heet N. Desai

AND I FOUND SOLACE

Amidst the green meadows I wander,
Hearing the chirping of melodious birds,
Peace is all that surrounds me,
And I can feel happiness without any efforts…

This river appears so clean and fresh,
Like it is flowing from the heaven above,
There's no stress here, no nuisance of any kind,
And I can truly sense nature's love…

There's no fan or a cooler here,
Nor a bed on which you can lie,
Just this sheet of grass to lay your body on,
And to cover your head is this magnificent sky…

When the long day ends and the night comes over,
This sky is decorated with a million stars,
A view that you can enjoy so care-freely,
There's no city crowd here, no horning of cars…

When this cool breeze of air touches my face,
I sense the presence of paradise,
This place seems so out of this world,
Beyond all virtues and vice..

If only life had given me a choice,
This is the place where I would spend all my nights and days,
Because such a peaceful life is just more than you can ask for,
And I won't be wrong in saying I had found solace...

As I was lying on the bed of grass,
Lost in my thoughts so deep,
A loud sound made its way into my ears,
And breaking of alarm drove me out of my sleep...

- Heet N. Desai

www.ingramcontent.com/pod-product-compliance
Ingram Content Group UK Ltd.
Pitfield, Milton Keynes, MK11 3LW, UK
UKHW041955190726
13854UKWH00005B/1996

9 789393 388339